Sanderlings

Also by Geri Doran

Resin

Sanderlings

Geri Doran

POEMS

T|P

Tupelo Press

North Adams, Massachusetts

Sanderlings

Library of Congress Cataloging-in-Publication Data

Doran, Geri, 1963–
Sanderlings : poems / Geri Doran. -- 1st pbk. ed.
   p. cm.
ISBN-13: 978-1-932195-95-8 (pbk. : alk. paper)
ISBN-10: 1-932195-95-5 (pbk. : alk. paper)
1. Faith--Poetry. I. Title.
PS3604.O73S36 2011
811'.6--dc22

2011007958

Cover and text designed by Josef Beery using the Adobe Garamond type family.
Cover art: "Untitled Fresco #12," 2008, by Mark Bennion (www.markbennion.com).
Used with permission of the artist.

First paperback edition: July 2011.
14 13 12 11 10   5 4 3 2 1

Printed in the United States.

 Supported in part by an award from
the National Endowment for the Arts

NATIONAL
ENDOWMENT
FOR THE ARTS

fellow travellers

Carolyn, Karen, David, David M.—
Jacob and C. Dale

and for Hilary

Contents

~

The Rounded Eyes of the Pagan God

Are exitways for the Soul—
and so the eyes half in awe, half-dazed
to house so great a magnanimity
never close.

Rock god with your look
of surprise, be calm. The Soul peers out
but rarely goes.

Sanderlings

This is the way the sand talks to me:
hush, hush. Whooshing along in the water's din.
Feet sunk in was how Mama said *hush.*

Sand says *no stone left unturned.* But sand
won't broach the Irish-green moss-covered rocks.
Further up, slick wet seal-colored rocks.

Then, dry rocks. Sand not willing but blown in.
Sand blown onto the A-beam legs of the pier
gets washed right back down.

Only a little's caught in the pocketed shells:
layers of barnacles crusting the pilings,
barely in sight at the waterline.

Fish-smell up on the pier. Fish in the water
calling to fish dying in buckets, saying *hush
redtail surfperch, hush starry flounder.*

So that you know I know their names.
Like the Asian men with their fishpoles know
the names. Or him down on the beach in hip-waders.

The other names here are white croaker, jacksmelt.
Sandpiper. Tern. *We gave you this name,*
Mama said, *for the saint who saved you.*

Starting out already in debt for life.
Hush, she only meant you should pray to him.
Instead of to the rocks and the sanderlings.

When the levee gave, the waves shot through.
Seawater soaked down to the roots
of the Monterey cypress and sent up ash.

That's the last detail, except for the sanderlings
chased up the beach by the waves
then skittering right back down into the wet.

Little sanderlings who never listen.
Tomorrow, when I return, my story will begin.

I, Putative

for Henri Cole

Barer than January maples, bare abandoned hives:
the bees silenced in their harvest rustle.
Like as to like, the soul
quiets, if soul it is, this bee box
in the chest. What outward presence
calls to inward space, *drop your wings?*
And what unclaimed interior complies?
Oh the flatland reveals its field of golden
stubble, and oh the sheared stalks
do not cry out. No, the chaff flutters
in the midland wind and the wings of the dead bees
quiver in the box.

Harrow

In the eyes of Dürer's St. Jerome,
desert inhabits the dark flecks
of his downward gaze.
It harrowed him. He came back clean
as picked bone. Chalcis of sunlight, and sand—
only in the eyes can days be counted,
days of muscle wasting, in which desire
dwindled to the body's dry growl.
He's written something for us—
the open page as luminous as his ancient beard
of golden white—but it's centuries now
and the hand's obscure.

~

To harrow: toil *after* the plow. It's spreading work,
once the deeper churning's done.
Always the smell of last year's crop,
roots long unquenched, then steeped
in sudden rain. The harrow's tracks
are as thin as the stomach's curse.
If time slowed till the finest dust
from each foot that met the rutted stair
were seen to cloud the shoe;
if the polished harrow on the museum floor
remained as mudcaked as the harrow

in memory; if, after centuries, particles
flourished like midges in the swarm
or wormed into the blond poles,
would the ground be ready for planting?
For we are hungry now,
says the farmhand to his dun-haired wife,
stretching up from the farm tableau. *Our desert
was also dry and flecked our eyes.*

The Dark Octaves

Germinal, the voice that within dirt
took root became the many-tendriled sound.
What haunts the ground haunts me, its ghostly art
to coil round where silence was, remand
quiet to the hum. Where words are indistinct
shut up where words *they can't* betray themselves—
indifferent contradictions, mouthed or inked.
No matter, we all betray ourselves, or loves.

    ~

Nothing, nothing to me. In turn I said:
two miles to the desert, ten miles to sea.
It was a conversation softly held, but held
beyond the going back. Under the lee
of the date palm and Bliss no more my consort,
I chose: sand-rider, camelback. My own
unnamed Sahara, the spoils X'd on a pirate
map: pisspot, halfpenny, psalter and crown.

    ~

Pisspot and crown. For once the nothing known
filled the pitcher to the brim. The O of O—
O wasted life—was colored in, the crown
atop the pot, a gold-plate aureole.

Sand, more sand, sable as burying clothes,
which wore away the calluses. Pleasure
reduced to this: the vocative, and sinking lows.
Foot-deep in it, a sand-trap made to measure.

~

Fevered, I plucked ripe fruit for its sweet smell.
Then briefed by hastening rot I stood
astute, finally, in the ways of field and bramble,
late berry juice on my tongue. My fingers wound
round the cloying branch, I pulled, wordless—
beanrows judged my crime behind the fence,
dispassionate and even. I cared far less.
The broken bough my sole, blue-tinged defense.

~

The mind recoils, believing not, believing
no vine could infiltrate this brick-on-brick
façade, its mortared keep. In-held, by evening
the mind itself splits. It's gorse by daybreak—
a tangled mass that fills the secret close.
No kissing bush, no lover's furze—it grows
prickers, thicketwise. Love stands cowering
outside the place that inside's self-devouring.

Impedimenta

The hackberry blackens in the March rain.
The bur oak in the backyard waits—
we are all out of season, unkind
in our distrait.

So say you, spring. So you said
one evening, cool, damp as this,
but disguised by veils of Spanish moss,
soaked and heavy. Every night
the same dream: hairline cracks
in the plaster wall, a lover seeping in.

Impassive fences corral green-brown
lawns. Reluctant, permeable skins.
The orange tabby permeates.
Makes her buttonhole stitch yard to yard.
A robin-redbreast mounts one fence,
then another. He is dividing his fire.

~

Out of season. April, perhaps, is crueler;
for now March is enough, these shoots
working up through hard layers.
The will is geologic: shale's density
commensurate with the desire
to withhold. Hardy crust, frozen
earth. Yet the tenderest green tips
nose into fissures and rise.

Out of this season comes the story.

~

Like no other. This is not rebirth,
nor the story of god and the devil
wagering at a barrio cockfight.
Especially this is not the truth.
It begins with a window, slightly raised,
that frames a barren tree,
home to a clutter of redwing blackbirds.
The birds which today are absent.

The window is a syllogism:
false logic on the nature of permeability.
If the window is closed it is impassable;
the window is open;
thus the soul disperses, fine-sieved
into black particulate with a small
red brushstroke on each wing.

~

Earth says, *come home. Darling,*
come down. Home is sky's
imperfect hesitation: cohesion
lost to an uptake of breath. Such loose
configuration of love,
such delicate meandering —

Earth stretches up
her grass-stained fingertips.

~

Or the blackbirds re-inhabit the hackberry,
and the tree in rain begins to bud,
buds to leaf, green feathering
the tree so as to camouflage, finally,
all weatherings of the soul.
So, you say. *Spring.*

~

There is no story, you understand.
Just foreplay in a dark March rain.

A Man Walks

Is it as simple, then, as picking up a seed?
The notion that art can be made from the chance
intervention of chestnut and gravity—
a man walking clear in the solitary blindness
of his responsibility
suddenly bends to wash his hand
through the litter of dropped pods until he finds
one perfectly split, the firm amber nut
protruding from the half-shell still enclosing it.
What does he do then but pocket the seed
and walk on with his blindness,
thumbing the velvet nub, learning
how the visibly smooth gives way to cranial bumps
under slight pressure—
In his field of vision now is a skull
under a thin, blue-veined transparence of skin;
this is memory, or portent—no convex mirror
of the right occluding and enhancing perspective,
nowhere even to view himself as himself—
just the stretch of skin
over the bones he was given at birth. It means
as little as the shower of red maple leaves
on his shoulders, a miniature curled one
stuck to the lapel of his worsted jacket
flicked carefully off.

How are we to proceed
in the advent of happenstance? Small decisions
made — *resolute* — in the morning light
brushed aside now with a flat palm.
The flicked leaf rises in the updraft
toward a seagull pulled slender by flight;
leaf and bird together
form a dashed line connecting nothing
in the pale air above the cement municipal building.
Yes, a seed fallen and claimed in the gap
is the accident he carries
as he walks,
as he will always walk,
a man abstractly bereft,
patrolling the small perimeter of his pause.

The Snowlit Sky

Thus prayer assails the unbeliever: a flush of white,
a stain in the imagination's night topography.
The black entanglements of the winter trees
form a darkness hemlocked, riverine—
quick rivulets arc, ascend, recede
into the looser, tilled surface of the night.
We open on territory uncomprehending
and vast: a ribboned dark, that choked branch
the length of Lear's unspent raving, deep as
the voice chastisement threw down
blow by blow onto the regrettable child
who wanted of Love . . . not this sermon.
In whom the hushed *nevertheless*
crimped a little tighter, the small-mouthed girl
gathering to herself such residues as were left.
This course in history is known and unsurprising,
the course of all small fiefdoms bent
on redemption but first and most cloyingly
on praise.

         What infirmity inheres? Likening it
to dry grass in the caked earth, is praise
mere succor, a trust of tears shed for the asking?
The wellspring chiefly the inheritance
of the trebly misunderstood: a shell game's
léger de main, not here, not here. The *earth's* not right—
the hillock's cursed; that plain blood-stained;
throughout, the starvelings are among us.
What's fealty next to this? Or, elsewhere—

The earth dispels its questions, rock
by rock. Pitch-black, the branches thicken night,
make a creek-bed of the blighted sky — one we follow,
lost to our geography, to reason, picking our way,
like a mad vainglorious king, and slipping wildly.

In the Valley of Its Saying

For there the heart lies beating beneath the articulate web,
its pulse no more than a blush on the flesh of the words.
The mouth bruised with elegy and dispraise of war,

no more is your mouth, nor his, nor poetry's own.
War and death have taken the mouth for their own.
For there the beat of the heart cracks quietly now, a rasp

like the cockroach's shell under the boot. Lebanon's run
to war, and Israel's run to war, and terror drips
down the chin of the world in a threadline of blood.

Blood on the mouth and blood on the tongue, Iraqi blood
shed under the watch of a televised world. Old ways.
Nothing written has caused one useless whit of change.

For there in the heart of its saying, its cracked and metered
saying, in its broken verse, poetry became the mouth
that couldn't speak: a mouth mouthing its silent curse.

Border Town

The present can't remember what it is.
—Larry Levis

Last night, rain fed the hundred lakes.
Bogland gave its watery tithe.
Now this river's urgency
professes a dual faith, one
streaming like avalanche-stone,
another milked up
through mud and grass. Water
runs to water, yes, but here
on the borderline,
what word will join them?
The bridge is worn stone
no doubt quarried
in the works near Carrickmacross.
Midway over are the old scars
where pylons kept
the loyalists out,
or the republicans out,
depending upon direction.

I am an American of Irish blood
who claims nothing
to speak of, my history erasable
with a quarter rag.
Nothing here's wiped away:
land primordial is scarred
and torn and what might be

forgotten is inscribed
in stone: a statue
commanding the village square
names three, dead fighting
the British Forces in '22,
Patrick Flood, William Kearney,
Bernard McCanny. A fourth,
William Deasley, of wounds
in the following days.

Across the Termon
the names are the same.
Thirty-feet-wide running high,
this river, poured-into
and rushing, slices
through a land
whole and wholly divided.
Schism road of water.
Pulpits of stone and warring.
Whose sermon cradles
the living, not just the dead boys
sluiced like tears
into their waiting graves?

Os Anjos

Martim Moniz, Lisbon

Daybreak of an autumn morning. I wake
to clattering: the rod that holds the oilcloth
that extends to cover the fruit in their wooden boxes.
Early shop-keeps stop for a cigarette,
smoke yeasting through damp overnight laundry
into sky. The city quickens with new arrivals:
voices rise in whispered urgencies—of Arabic,
the *crioulos*—and rising grasp the ledge *safe harbor*
and hold. Verging like the angles of the orange rooftops,
we are a field of intersecting planes. This one
is sloping tiles. That, green tarp covering the seam.
The Ukranian girl in her low-slung jeans is an aerial.
She receives men, leads them buzzing
to an open door along the Poço do Borratém.

        Verging like angels, like angels
caught pigeoning the streets: dingy and plucking
their plumage. We roost in damage and filth,
root in filth, are angels, pocked feathers, are dreadlocks,
cooks and squatters, minders of shops, are fallen,
angels and girls.

Pigeon

Victor of filth: flinging lettuce-husk, your province flag,
in the L-shaped ingress of the *Frutaria*. This ground
you take from aboveworld, your vantage
a rotting sill. Dirtybird, with your neck-thrust walk
and orangeade eyes, now you sit so blankly still
in the window, cracked glass your portrait-frame.
Dirtybird, harbinger of citymorning, hallower of grime,
greybird, pluckbird, O bring us your sunup,
your percolating tut of day.

Summer Is Sweet and Long

Budapest, 2006

Summer is sweet and long, the evening a jingling bicycle bell—
here I come. It is hours yet till dark. It is decades since the last
occupation and along the avenue people in the cafés are laughing.
There is almost nothing to mourn; the weatherman calls for blue skies
and the puffiest white clouds soften the pointiest steeples
on the starch Hapsburg monoliths. Evening clanging her bell,
dahlias and freesia in the basket that were handpicked
this morning by the Roma grandmother and sold in Astoria station
for next to nothing. She brought them in her plaid-sided cart.
Under the lenient sun, a church has begun to chime
the later o'clocks, as if the clerics in their heavy cassocks
wished to join in the revelry, because even studious clerics
revel sometimes, and do so by ringing.

The Atlantis of Morning

Dear Wanderer,

The beachcombers are in want of an elegy,
and you are peddling starlight.

Where is the music in this?

The water is making its usual sound
against the usual rocks, and the Golden Gate Bridge

stands unswinging above its blue bath.

The beachcombers have begun their slow-hipped pivot,
stretching down for the solace of reaching.

~

I was mistaken.

The beach is an elegy for want, and you,
wanderer, have abandoned your stars

which want for nothing but presence.
At sunrise, willing to lapse

back into the light of an oncoming day.

~

Call it The Breakers, The Headlands—
this strand of earth shaped by water

is as derelict as the gulls. Their cries
amended by wind into one stark tracing of a cry.

Call it simply *vantage:* the point
of view into which Atlantis rises again

in a different ocean.

~

Atlantis is an old-world story of passion, nothing more.
A city guarded by sea, a jealous god,

the usual sins of fallible men. Mainly, there is the storm.
The storm, and ever after the mystery

of what lies underwater, the mystery
the beachcombers try to solve

for the solace of trying.

~

Have you never grown tired of metaphor,
its making and remaking

the insufficient world into a tenable one.
Its likening of this to that.

~

Even desire. Even that has the pattern

of want, not want. The water cups the earth
and shudders back.

Atlantis II

Disgorgement: this refusal of the sea
to swallow and hold down the lies that vein
subfloor and walls, an endoskeleton
of "would you like" and "yes I would please"
when all that's meant is "no" and "no"
when civility's as friable as asbestos
in the tile.
         This is what the ocean ate,
with a side of seaboats run to wreck
by sirens — those sea nymphs of the Waterside Café,
their sea cousins in every coastal town,
small-breasted, with a little extra flesh
around the thighs, their land cousins
regular at Maxine's Beauty Shop,
faces pink from the drying hoods —
it ate the burg, the cotton field, the crown
of Crown Point, the river salmoning past,
it ate the Westside Highway
and SeaTac's north terminal, this ocean
ate the tall buildings and the low-riders,
the vinyl siding, the slip of paper
on which someone had written in an angry hand
"RT — I won't forget this" tucked behind the wall
and puttied over, puttied and painted over,
it ate promises that veined the boards
like fishnet. Then it tossed them back.

Aubade

for Carolyn Altman

At sunrise, the stars lapse back into the light
of day, that onrush of bright

we call, with reverence, *morning*—
hearing the echo of something lost.

Their lit particularity framed by dark
is a form of love.

What the stars have by night
we reach for in words, by day,

mourning not for the thing, or the lack—
mourning the distance we must travel to get it.

Let me push through the rubble:
buckets of sand, a broken sand dollar,

useless currencies of the manifest world.
If I say solace, I mean the sharp chunk of seawall

bracing the cliff. By starlight I mean
an Atlantis of meadow-flowers surrounded by water

sinking back into the blue.

The Landlocked Girl's Tale

One day he burned the shanties down.
Lit the field. Already I loved
the darkened carcass, the shell
that was a shell before the burn. Disaster
begins before we ever guess.

Four shanties' emptiness. The field, lit,
the chaff's dull gold turning black.
How not to burn again? How not transform
this readiness? My body's a field afire,
another shack-town, going up.

Building in the City of Lath and Plaster

We lay a grid against the framing wall, nail splintered wood to the studs. Every inch, a slat parallel to the horizon. Over the slats, a lathering of plaster coral of corals, or the pink of sea anemone. Roughed in, filled out—we craft our framework of promises: the lath *will* hold; the plaster adhere to the lath. When the plaster draws away, its fingerhooks cling. A provision against outright separation.

Cleito to the Landlocked Girl

Fire? A woman's sooner wrecked by water.
Poseidon's caress: at first a little something
under the dress, then twin sons
five times over. My island crammed
with boys. Look at my Dionysian darlings,
drunk on mother-love.
        Poseidon doesn't visit anymore.
Just to see them. An evening's talk
around the hearth — statesmanship and kings,
this rule, that bit of commerce with the Greeks.
My people, once. I am undone.
And not undone: no more
his tracings at my shore. Nor my body's
lift and give, transformed to water
by water's hand. Yours is a field-song
crackling down to ash. *This* is the sound
of the ebbing wave: a lone gull's cry
becoming wind.

Atlantis III

I mean to describe the city, this city.
      It was an island of bellflowers once.

Atlantis IV

Consider earth, alternating with rings of water. The difficulty
in mapping this. Is it one island — or several? Consider the accretion
of houses, brick and mortar massing behind the old vines. Then, this
house: a practical matter of shelter, and warmth, and the formal
arrangement of lumber along the ligaments of desire. Rough-hewn lath.
Its overlay of coral. Wherein arises a question, whether island differs
from city, building from the material that makes it. And so, what
signifies lying, when one thing is so like another? Consider myth:
the woman at its center. She is not singing. Water cupping the earth
is *singing*, but in human form we cannot hear its cadence. We reach
down, and over, and we fail.

The Storm in Solace

O Atlantis.

                O city burdened by water.
The beachcombers have arrived for the mystery.

Have you left it here with the broken shells?

~

Ebb-tide, the name we give it.
One stands on the breakers, the other

is elsewhere at the water's edge, pivoting
down, and something in their solitary stance

reminds us of a city lost in a single torrent.

The expanse before, and stretching out forever
afterward, was the bright cerulean blue

of a painter's palette.
                Was blue, and quiet.

The Atlantis of Morning (Reprise)

Dear Wanderer,

Do not abandon me to the sourcelight of words.
They are like stars, lapsing back

just as the sun comes over the Golden Gate.

What of this water's inconstant desire
can I take for granted? My ways are inland.

I take one rock, and another, and another—
to build a fire in the salt-licked air.

There is no chaff here for burning.
There is only the tide, its habit of vanishing.

And out toward the horizon, a city
like any of our cities

also vanishes.

Thy belly is like a heap of wheat set about with lilies.
SONG OF SONGS, 7:2

City

First morning, I woke
to the lying-downness of myself: my alabaster
arm and thigh more silken rampart,
my curves their hills, and in my dew-wet bed
of grass, I knew that my geography
would become terrain, and from terrain
sweet mappable streets. I am through-country
and settle.
They knew it, too —

men broaching my embankments, the toll
little enough: ruby trinket, coin.
So they paid, and in paying filled
their cups. Filled the cups
and stayed,

eager pigeons flocking to my line
and pecking, pecking.
No if I call them city rats, then I am dirty
city, squalid city, teeming
along corridors of outer darkness.

Lies, it's lies. Venality's
no charge for beauty's exacting
recompense.

~

This my tribunal: a court of fire.
Jury of licking flames, white-hot judge
stoking the coals.
He trails his verdict along my thigh
and chars my skin.

~

You call me Babylon, call me Whore—
I am Mystery and that name comes
before all other names.
If my accuser is a trinity, then so am I,
city, woman, and the one that
is the three.

Talk, talk—you think that it reveals.
Talk is my privacy.
If I talk until oblivion do you think
you will know anything? Dear men,
you copulate.
After, you are as virginal
as the hundred and forty-four thousand
lambs, his bleating followers.
For these did not know women.

~

Remember
what I was? Sweet territory,
meadow of dahlias
full to bursting. I was summer.
The field that sprang
at the end of the street of the shoemakers,
beyond the leather-tanners' lane.
I was footpath
I was forest
I was love.

~

Easy, now. Rains are falling,
scattering dirty drops on windows.
City is a mottled view,
dabbed with pigeon scum and streaks
of paint.

One skyrise sees itself
in the windows of another.
So we look onto ourselves,
and what we see is glassy, bent.

~

We needed no translators.
Birds chirping
in our thousand tongues.
All perched together
on the highwires, the curbs.

Now they name me *a hold of foul spirit.*
If I *am* befouled,
who will pity me?
Not the new converts. O rapture me,
they cry.

O seize my plain, pluck my
searocks for paving stones, dig
clay for wall, coal for fire,
diamond for selling,
root for knowledge.
I did not say: take all, except this fruit.
I said: take all, and take some more—

until I was bejeweled
with lampposts and iron pheasants
curving above shop doors,
marquees and limelight,
my alabaster arms
sheathed in silk

streaked now with char.

The Passion of Mary, Called Magdalene

Matter gave birth to a passion that has no equal

As if the dead quiet of the stalled wind. As if
That last, riven breath before air changes is you.
Sky is inside you, parting. Sky is outside, you
Cannot take in enough of it. That which you will
Never get enough of begins in your own body. It is
Of body, falling earthward.

In the time before my ardor, men would lay
Their silver pieces down, entering in just the way
A sail catches the wind, larger than itself, professing
Mastery of its direction. Each would enter
And I would be the stalled air, thinking
This is your beggar's compromise.

For silver, for the feel of new linen I would be
That stilled expectancy, counting coins as they left.
In the aeon before, body was merely body,
My waiting a ruse. Alone I was a skyful
Of snow, its soft arousal. Alone humming
Snowfall is the self's first bewilderment.

And desire said, I did not see you descending

No, entranced by the snowfall, I did not see.
He came to me cloaked in it, so whitely. As if
A shimmer of petals warming to water on my face.
Breathing I took in more than air, I took in
Him, and the luminous cells in me parted.

Ever after, when he spoke the word *chaste*
I was blizzarded. He entered, not as blown sail,
But as himself, a man causing the earthward
Freefall of snow, a descent white-blinded,
In-taken, bodied. *Adoramus te, Christe.*
Adoro te.

In an aeon, I was released from a world

Adoro meaning your words fall through the length
Of me so that I am the birth of listening.
The words, the listening, the body
Inseparable. For I have been the riven air
And been sewn clean with a word.

He said, *Do you hear what I name you?*
I hear, my snowfall, my sweet
bewilderment.

GERI DORAN

The Good Field

Because in the heat-drenched night an angel prevailed. Into her belly, he said.
Into her life a shimmer, drawn like satin drapery over her breast. She heard this
in her dream, its echo rustling under the day's water-bearing and washing
until sun's rest, a voice as ardent as blue dahlias casting off their petals.
Foundling,

said the angel, this now, your belly, swollen into the bright foregift of martyrdom,
this shall mean *bounty;* sheaves of wheat on your dress will be the everlasting mark
of your sweet and fertile entailment. She must have heard this, couldn't have mistaken
dahlias for a slip of wind or Joseph's breath, in and further in, for it is true that
the faded muslin

of her day-dress was embroidered now with stalks of wheat, just as the angel had said,
and that the painters, when they came, all those centuries later, to paint her, divined
the dress, knew to render her plump, the fine lines near her mouth fleshed out, her belly
already a small rise when she slept and a shallow bowl for her hand when she bent
at the well.

Beatific, the look the painters would give her, and later, after all the trials, still
picturing her full and fertile and now dolorous—that was their word—the dolor
of Mary, mother of Jesus, when rage is what it was, those spots of red in her cheek.
Not some bright and dovetailed sadness but an always-impending bounty bought with
a heavenly chit.

So she was ample, and still young at the cross, Mary, broken mother of Jesus, mothering
a son matted with blood and straw and trying, all of them trying, to make it *mean*
something. That's the part the painters leave out, how each time the sun ascended towards
God she would say, let us be done today, no one imagining a mother wishing that,
wishing even

death if it meant, finally, an end to a bounty so unfailingly meager it was no more
than an empty furrow in an empty field, not the promised harvest, nothing shimmering
or silkening the years, just the cold hard fact of corporeal love. Foundling, said the angel.
Foundling, would you do it again? A ploughed field stares up at a parched sky.
Mary the dolorous

mother of God, Mary the good field waiting. Not bounty but its unrelenting prospect,
the womanly belly with its rounded, wheat-colored swell, the stalks bending
in the windborne breath of heaven, and scattered among the sheaves the long, tapering
stems of the pure-white lilies of the valley, their small bells ringing quietly, ringing *yes,*
ringing *always.*

Earth Moving

So near, the tide cracks. We are four
birds on the bank above. We watch
with worry for the man moving

riprap up the beach. He has lost
nothing, has gripped each rock
roundly and swung. We nose

among the pilings, gathering words
to share, here, here—
we are lonely birds.

~

High tide so near the treaded belts
so near to swimming the excavator
out to sea. Mid-afternoon, it

tips forward into the devil's froth,
tips back. The boulder in its jaw
is a counterweight. *Speak with*

your eyes, bird says to bird.
The words in my mouth are rocks
I mumble through.

~

At the edge of this fidgeting world.
At swim in the devil's broth.
Bird to bird.

The man at his lever lifts himself
high with the bucket, lifts himself
and the machine high up—

so sand washes in under the treads.
For something stable to rest on.
For nothing is lost, that way.

Tabula Rasa

Enter into testimony: the name *Beloved.*
An inmost calm cannot abide in this.
As I am often told —
the long walk by the roaring sea
the long walk roaring by the sea
made not unknowing nor without cease

yet planed smooth along the corded vein —
though sand be not the sculpted grain, nor wood,
though walking be not grieving, nor the plane.

Common Prayer

Stirring among the pines. The sapling's leaves
like oval wings tremble. Between the whoofs
of startled deer, echoing, an echoing clear
creed of some unvanquished mystery —
night-rising crows humbling their caws
below the oaky whoo of the boreal owl.
Below that, what? Threads of wood,
a bed of pine, the needles strewn in love
beside a creek itself so prodigal
we dare not drink before the water's moved,
trestling over the rocked and craggy bed.

   (adoration)

Beloved, says the paper birch, *I err*
against the very air, and cannot sleep.
For in sleep the foul self inaugurates,
cathedral-like, a plan: to cast pardon
skyward stone on stone, enclosing grace
within the higher arches of the marble dome,
and thence to pray, thence to pray — *You are*
scaffold, stairstep, oak-creak, tarn — I am
never worthy — Your sincerest kneeling knave.

   (contrition)

Alas, earnestness and candor fill the trees
and wisdom creaks like floorboards underfoot:
a silence remaining silent until pressed
by wind or weight, and what of discretion's
wiser counsel, to bear the weight and sigh
so quietly the angels do not hear;
and this is love, my child, remember this —
I speak to you with love; but love, I do not
always speak.

  (charity)

O my most fragrant Lord, you are honeysuckle
my childish hand will not relinquish. Forbear,
this once, your punishment of lilac and rose —
for in this wild and weedlike trickery
I am made meadowless.

  (petition & intercession)

For God is only God in the Marsden Rock.
Love permits his echo be dispersed
among the trees, and merely echo, and mere —
what concentrates is silt beneath the creek,
the residue of love after time has closed
its doors and hung the sign —
for we are scorners all and yet may know
that love which tidepools us,
like sea anemone in coastal caves.

  (grace)

Notes and Acknowledgments

Lines and poems in this collection pay homage to essential predecessors, among them W. H. Auden, Elizabeth Bishop, Henri Cole, Seamus Heaney, Brigit Pegeen Kelly, Larry Levis, Robert Lowell. What thanks to give but in the poems?

"I, Putative." The title is a phrase from Henri Cole's poem "Jealousy."

"In the Valley of Its Saying." From the original version of "In Memory of W. B. Yeats." Auden later revised the line to "in the valley of its making."

"Border Town." The statue occupies the village square in Pettigo, County Donegal. Epigraph is from "Elegy with the Sprawl of a Wave Inside It" by Larry Levis.

"City." Italicized text is adapted from The Book of Revelations.

"The Passion of Mary, Called Magdalene." Section headings are excerpts from the "Gospel of Mary [Magdalene]," one of three Gnostic scriptures discovered in Egypt in 1895. See the online collection of the Gnostic Society Library.

"The Good Field." Inspired by "O Brilho das Imagens," an exhibition at the Museu National de Arte Antigua, Lisbon, of fifteenth-century Silesian works on loan from the national museum in Warsaw. Two paintings in particular were instructive in their pictorial and Biblical representations of Mary as the "Madonna of the Ears of Wheat" and her appellation as "The Good Field."

"Tabula Rasa." For Karen Ford and Laurie Lynn Drummond.

"Common Prayer." For G. C. Waldrep.

~

I am grateful to the editors of the following journals, where these poems first appeared, sometimes in other versions:

Image: "Common Prayer" and "Harrow"; *New England Review:* "The Atlantis of Morning (Reprise)," "Earth Moving," and "The Good Field"; *The New Republic:* "I, Putative," "Pigeon," and "The Rounded Eyes of the Pagan God"; *Ninth Letter:* "Tabula Rasa"; *Poetry International:* "The Snowlit Sky"; *Southern Review:* "Summer Is Sweet and Long"; *Southwest Review:* "The Passion of Mary, Called Magdalene" and "Sanderlings"; *The Stinging Fly:* "Border Town"; *Subtropics:* "The Dark Octaves"; *TriQuarterly:* "The Atlantis of Morning," "City," and "Impedimenta."

"Earth Moving" also appears in Enskyment, an online anthology (www.enskyment.org).

~

For the inestimable gift of travel, my continuing thanks to the trustees of the Amy Lowell Poetry Travelling Scholarship. One year transforms a lifetime. My gratitude also to Bread Loaf Writers' Conference and Vermont Studio Center for generous fellowships; and to the Oregon Humanities Center and College of Arts and Sciences at the University of Oregon for kind support of the *Sanderlings* audio disk. Michael Madonick and Karen Ford read early versions of this book, generously and insightfully; and the fine folks at Tupelo Press—especially my editor, Jim Schley—are remarkable in their abiding belief in poetry. My thanks to them, and to my dear friends and family, named at the start and beloved till the end.

OTHER BOOKS FROM TUPELO PRESS

* Also available as a Tupelo audio book
See our complete backlist at www.tupelopress.org